# A Wild & Wonderful West Virginia Alphabet

Dena L. Beckner

**For my wild & wonderful friends and family with all my love and gratitude.**

Text and illustrations copyright © 2023 by Dena L. Beckner

All rights reserved. No part of this book may be used or reproduced in any way whatsoever without written permission from the author except in the case of brief quotations embodied in critical articles or reviews.

First published by author in Davis, West Virginia

Typeset in Recoleta.
The art was created by hand using pencil and watercolor.

ISBN-979-8-218-96991-2

"The sun doesn't always shine in West Virginia, but the people do."
-John F. Kennedy

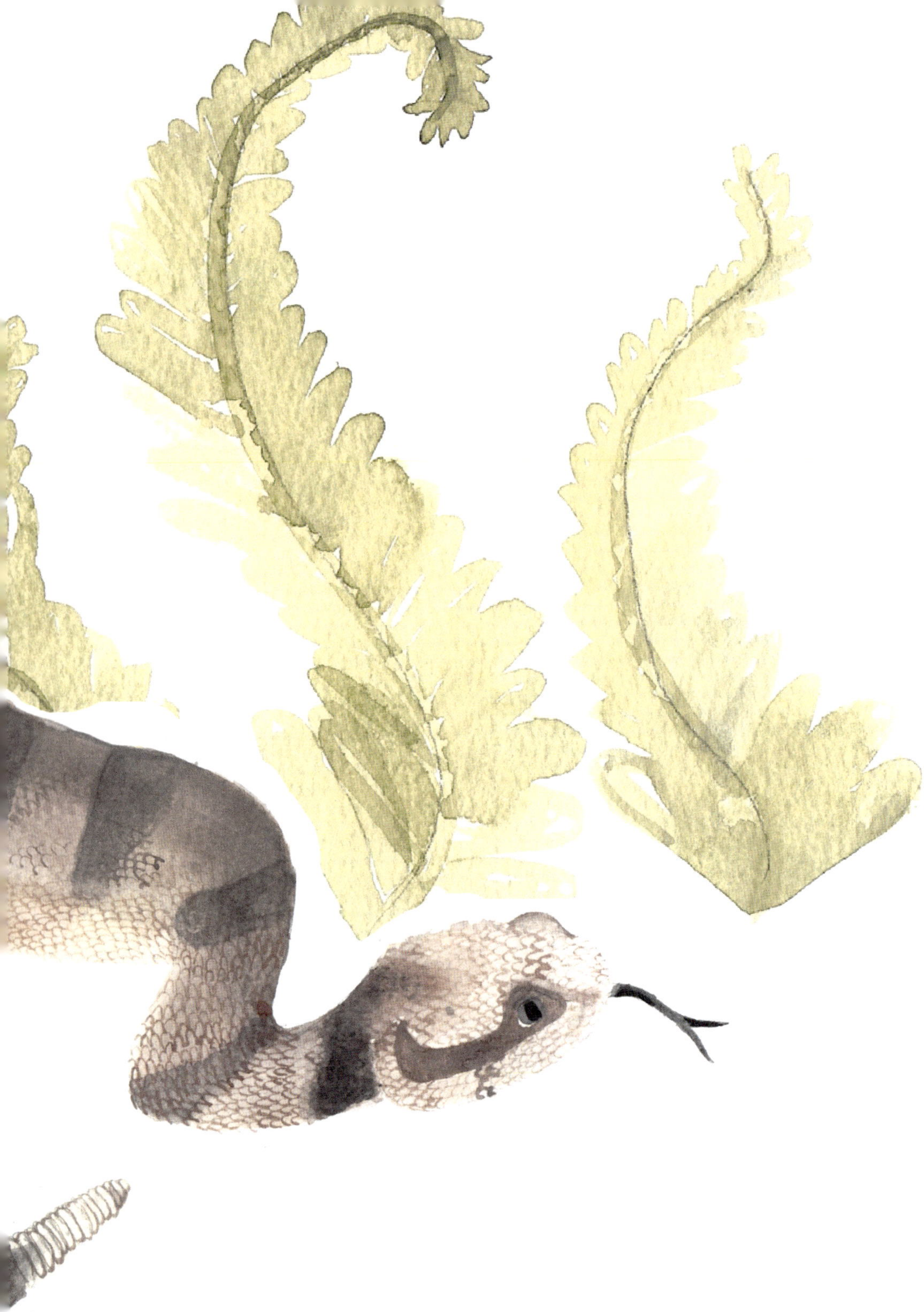

This book belongs to:

# A is for Appalachian Mountains.

The **Appalachian Mountains** are a mountain range located in the eastern United States. West Virginia is the only state that lies entirely within the Appalachian Mountain region.

# B is for brook trout.

West Virginia's state fish is the **brook trout**. It is known for its earthy coloring, pale wormlike markings, and affinity for cold mountain streams.

# C is for cardinal.

The West Virginia state bird is the northern **cardinal.** The cardinal is a non-migrating songbird with a crested head. The male cardinal is vibrant red with a coal black face. The female is pale brown with light brushes of red.

# D is for deer.

The **white-tailed deer** can be found everywhere in West Virginia. It has a white underbelly and a white tail that stands up when frightened. Males shed and regrow their antlers every year.

# E is for elderberry.

**Elderberry** is a native plant to West Virginia that produces fragrant white flowers and clusters of tiny purple inky berries.

# F is for fiddlehead fern.

**Fiddlehead ferns** are the curled fronds of young ferns that sprout up in early spring in the wooded hills of West Virginia.

# G is for golden delicious apple.

The **golden delicious apple** was discovered in West Virginia and is the state fruit. It has a very sweet flavor and is great for eating raw or baking into a pie.

# H is for honey bee.

The **honey bee** is the West Virginia state insect. The honey bee is very important for pollination and is the only bee species that makes honey.

# I is for infamous mothman.

The legend of the **infamous mothman** describes a flying insect-like creature with large wings and red, glowing eyes. He likes peace signs and black-eyed susans.

# J is for John Henry.

**John Henry** is an American Folk Hero who was "born with a hammer in his hand." Legend says that he battled a steam powered driller in a challenge of man versus machine at the Great Bend Tunnel in West Virginia. His strength and determination ultimately defeated the machine.

# K is for Katherine Johnson.

**Katherine Johnson** was a West Virginia native who worked as a human computer for NASA and whose math helped spacecrafts and astronauts enter into orbit and ultimately land on the moon.

# L is for lightning bug.

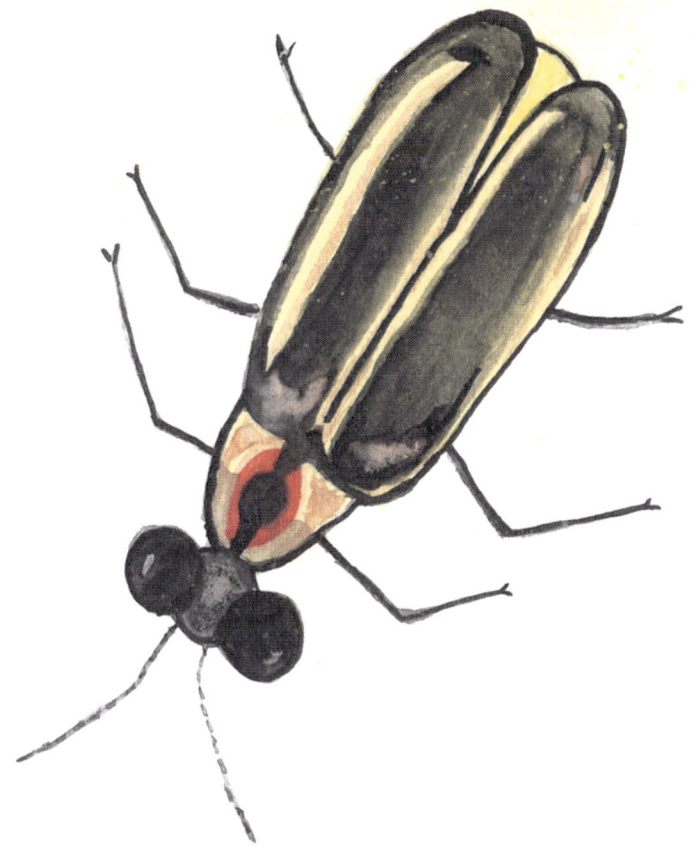

**Lightning bugs** are flying beetles whose light-emitting abdomens speckle the evening summer sky.

# M is for monarch butterfly.

The **monarch butterfly** is the West Virginia state butterfly. The monarch feeds solely on the milkweed plant. Each year, the monarch population migrates from Mexico up through North America and back to Mexico again.

# N is for northern red salamander.

The **northern red salamander** is the West Virginia state amphibian. It enjoys cool mountain streams in wooded habitats. Salamanders are a great indicator of local environmental health because they're very sensitive to surrounding stressors.

# O is for Olympian Mary Lou Retton.

**Olympian Mary Lou Retton** is a West Virginia native who became the first American woman to win the all-around Olympic gold medal in gymnastics.

P is for pepperoni rolls.

**Pepperoni rolls** are the unofficial West Virginia state favorite food. The pepperoni roll consists of a baked bread stuffed with pepperoni and sometimes cheese.

# Q is for quilt.

A **quilt** is an heirloom blanket that is composed of assorted fabrics stitched together in patterns. You can find quilt squares painted on barns across West Virginia.

# R is for rhododendron.

The **rhododendron** is an evergreen shrub and the West Virginia state flower. In the late spring to early summer, the shrub produces large and vibrant purple, pink, or white blossoms.

# S is for sugar maple.

The **sugar maple** is the West Virginia state tree and the primary source of maple syrup.

# T is for timber rattlesnake.

The **timber rattlesnake** is a venomous pit viper and the West Virginia state reptile. It is known for the tail rattling warning it gives when threatened.

# U is for underground coal mining.

**Underground coal mining** is a long-established industry in West Virginia, in which coal miners dig underground to extract black coal that is used to produce energy.

Bituminous "black" coal is West Virginia's state rock.

# V is for Virginia big-eared bat.

The **Virginia big-eared bat** is an endangered species with extremely large ears. It is found only in West Virginia, Virginia, Tennessee, and North Carolina.

# W is for wild ramps.

The **wild ramp** is a wild onion with a potent garlicky onion flavor. It is found in the forests of West Virginia during the spring.

# X is for fo**x**.

West Virginia is home to the red **fox** and the gray fox. The fox is a dog species, but it has similarities to cat species, such as retractable claws.

# Y is for Chuck Yeager.

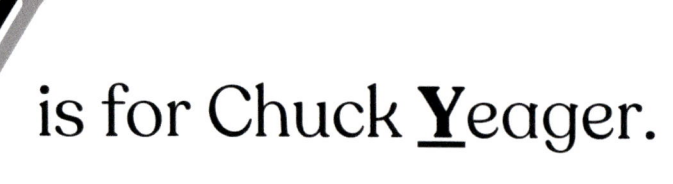

**Chuck Yeager** is a West Virginia native and the first person to break the sound barrier in 1947 when he flew his aircraft faster than the speed of sound.

# Z is for zucchini.

The **zucchini** is a large, green summer squash vegetable that is grown abundantly in West Virginia and enjoyed in a variety of culinary dishes.

# Other important West Virginia facts:

- West Virginia was proclaimed a state in 1863.

- West Virginia's nickname is "The Mountain State."

- West Virginia Day is celebrated on June 20th.

- The state motto is "Montani Semper Liberi" which means, "Mountaineers Are Always Free."

- The state mammal is the black bear.

- The state colors are old gold and blue.

- The state fossil is the Jefferson ground sloth.

- The state gem is Silicified Mississippian Fossil Coral.

- The highest point in the state is Spruce Knob.

- The lowest point in the state is Harpers Ferry.

**State of West Virginia**

**Montani Semper Liberi**

*Mountaineers are always free!*

# Field Notes:

# Field Notes:

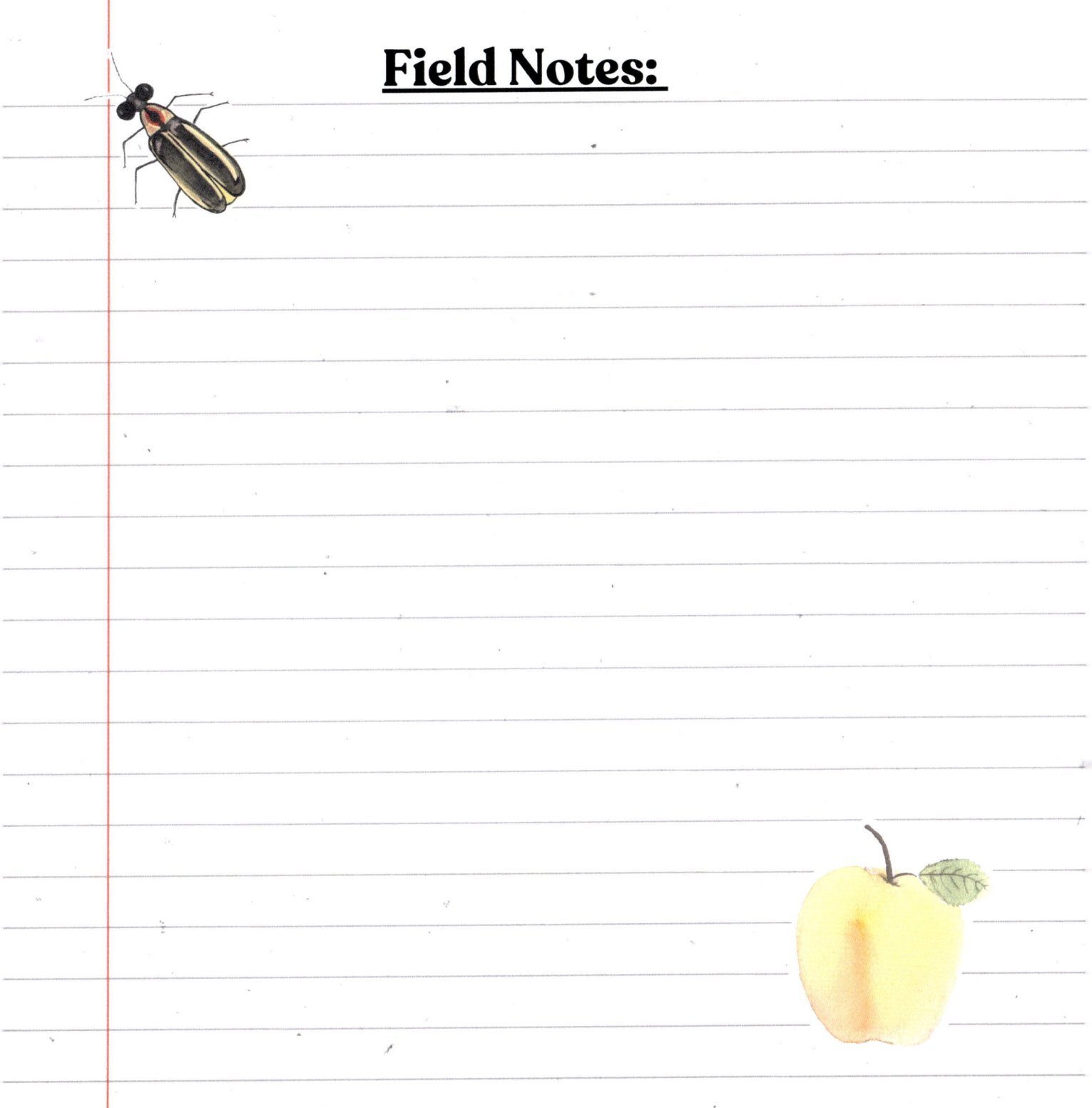

# Field Notes:

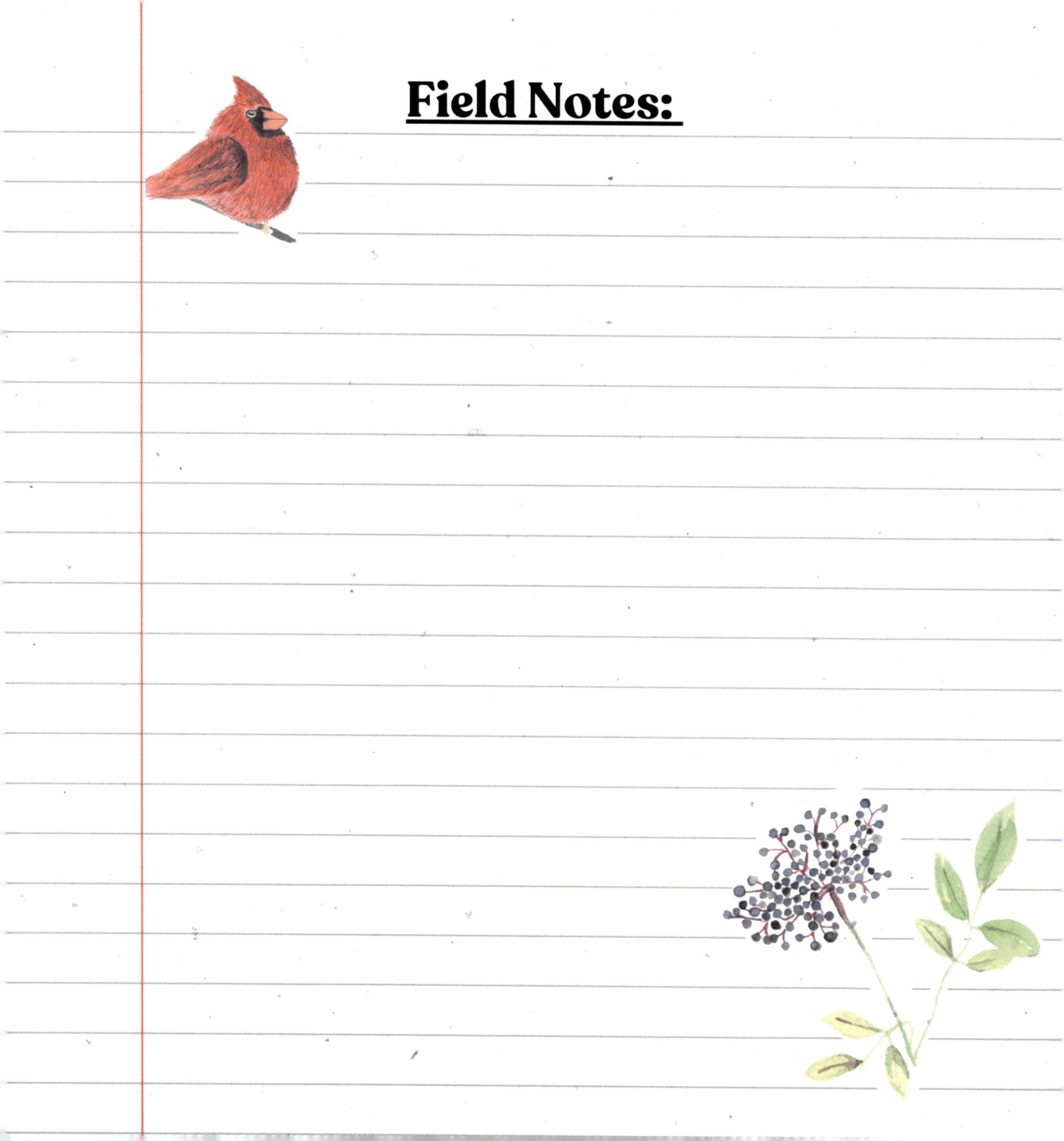

## Field Notes:

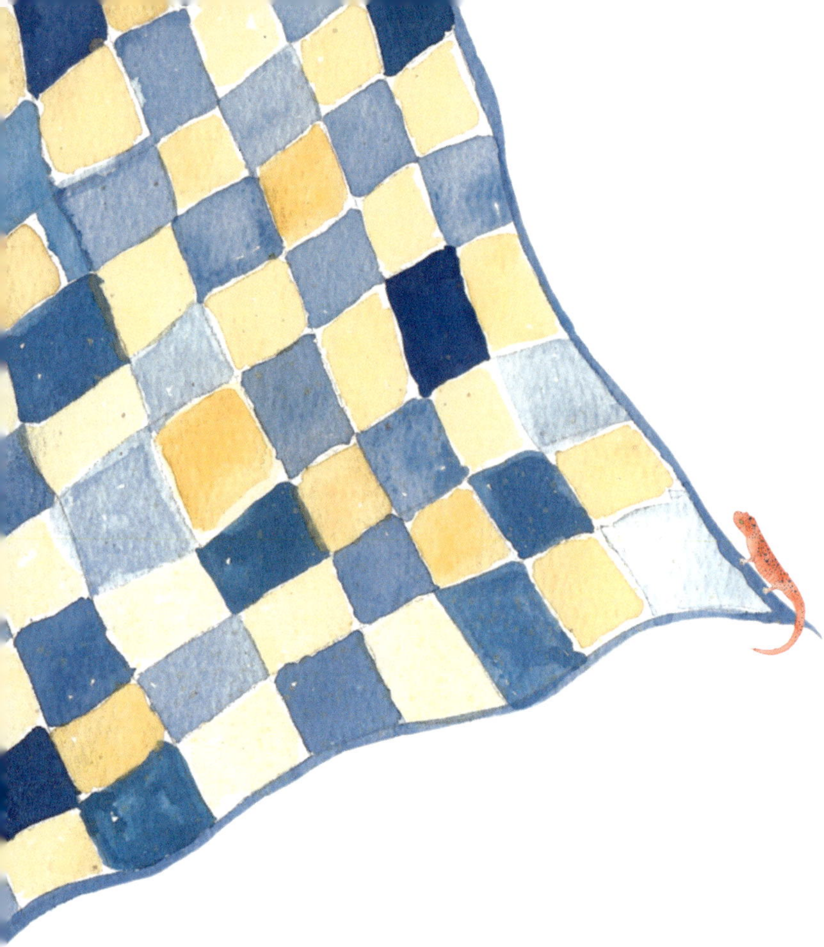

Dena was born and raised in the rural mountains of West Virginia. She spent her childhood running barefoot through the woods, chasing lightning bugs and crawdads, swimming in cold mountain water, and picking wildflowers and blackberries.

Nowadays, she still enjoys the wild beauty the state has to offer. When she isn't adventuring in Tucker County with her husband and three children she can be found working as a Physician Assistant in rural family medicine.

This book was created as a passion project out of her deep love for her forever home, West Virginia.

"For you shall go out in joy, and be led back in peace; the mountains and the hills before you shall burst into song, and all the trees of the field shall clap their hands."
- Isaiah 55:12

Made in the USA
Middletown, DE
28 November 2024